Evergreen Heart Chronicles

Samantha Cimber Perez

BookLeaf Publishing
India | USA | UK

Presentation by *BookLeaf Publishing*

Web: www.bookleafpub.com

E-mail: info@bookleafpub.com

ISBN: 9789357443647

First edition 2022

DEDICATION

This book is dedicated to every dreamer that works to bring forth their creativity. I hope you find reasons to move swiftly in kindness and love.

ACKNOWLEDGEMENT

Thank you to all my loved ones that encourage me to follow my dreams.

PREFACE

In peaceful moments- that is when she finds it.
A driving force to speak to herself kindly.
Surrendering to each new step.
Understanding it is all meant for a brilliant
experience.

The Lost Girl

A lost girl will read a person's soul because it is addictive.
She gets lost in the things that were inflicted.
She will be a mirror and a projection of things that are not clear.
She sways with the vibrational pull that is near.
She will not ask if any of it is real.
She gets lost in the fear and calls it hope.
She loves just for the hell of it.
The void in her heart is an uncomfortable place.
She lets her discord define her because she could not regulate how to experience her own being.
She has watched bodies turn into stone not knowing how to give more.
In her hurt she ran... or did she?
There is mud between her toes and that is a bit of a mystery.
But she could have sworn there was a fall.
With all the different moves- she slips into her heart.
That is where the story starts.

The Jaguar

Woke up to the ground scratch against her
shoulder blades.
Eyes open to the trees that touch the ether.
The ache in her chest vibrated through her.
How falling can be so reflective and leading
with love can be so rejected.
Fate and destiny called her differently.
It was choosing her to be awake in her lucid
mind.
Selfish?
I'd say that is a bit too much.
But she dreamt of this moment nonetheless.
Where she was on the inside of her fearless
heart.
The pain in that being truly unearthly.
Trust is important and she discorded it.
That floor never felt so fortunate and tears of
defeat never tasted so sweet.
In the reaction to her body breaking, she felt the
presence of another being.
She felt the dew of his snout at the center of her
forehead.
His breath exchange restarted her circuit.
His piercing gaze gave her presence and reason.
He laid alongside her body.

His gray and black fur bestowed warmth.
She rolled over to hold his life in her arms.
A bond never felt so simple.
His unconditional love was a reason to feel.
To place her bare feet upon the earth; stabilizing
herself in this new life she prayed for with her
new friend by her side-
FREEDOM BECAME HER.

The Spirit of the Bear

She spotted the spirit of the bear and followed downstream.
Doing her best not to fall behind especially in her disbelief at what she was seeing.
The soul of her friend that held her whole truth.
"Is he alive?," she thought.
She felt weak but prayed not to wake.
If this was a lucid trance, she understood the blessing of the chance.
Still incapable of speaking, she let her reverent energy explain to her company how precious this was.
She acknowledged he was sent to show her love.
His patience sensed as she climbed over logs.
Finally, they halted by the bank.
The bear instructed her and the jaguar to step into the river.
Before she entered, with her mouth trembling, she decided to speak: "I wish you were coming with us my friend."
The kind animal nudged her in and then stated, "we will meet again."
She laid into the water with her jaguar by hand.

A memory had clicked and in that moment she realized the transfer between two familiars was complete.

She sailed on her emotions.

The thought came as quickly as it went:

"There is more to come in this strange hallowed land."

The Gentle Soul

That is when she recalled- her whole world
shifted.
The weight of the current pulled her in a state of
remembrance.
A time where she felt lonely for being unseen.
Maybe that was the projection of her being.
She wanted so much change but continued to
stay the same.
She recognized that she was in love with her
pain so she began to explore it.
Asked herself the big thoughts but the Gentle
Soul in him chose his innocence.
He paid her with patience for her time.
He had an even tempered mind.
He had to- that is how he grew.
His favorite thing to do was to play.
He never wanted to be wrong.
And they both knew they did not know how to
stay.
How to stay in love with themselves and each
other.
There is no one to blame because that is only
the aim when you treat others like a game.
That is what she did: she tried to fix something
that was always just missing.

He let her because an innocent love helped
create her.
An innocent love forgave her.
That innocent love holds her in a position where
she finds recognition in her being.
It is a love she is grateful to experience.
She believes he will pick a life with peace in it
daily.
That is what God gave her.
A beautiful love to hold her when she was weak.
To hear him say, "It is okay, I am still your
friend today."
He loved her even when she admitted that is all
she wanted to be.
Her heart grew so much bigger and that is
because there is no lack of love for a man that
helped her find her way.
"Forgiveness," she thought as she let her head be
held by the stream, "I will drink it in one day."

The North Star

Her favorite was the night sky.
Even in the dark she knew she was not lost.
It was the beautiful North Star that would help
her find her way.
As she relaxed in the current she had little fears
because the shining rock was near.
The current pulled her towards it- as if she was
swimming in a galaxy.
She always felt that the North Star was made
just for her.
The guide and constant in her life that reminds
her of home.
When she closes her eyes she imagines the
beautiful sphere of light smiling just for her.
That Star has been her wanderlust since the day
she discovered its existence.
The North Star is endlessly tattooed onto her
soul.
Because of this engraving she knows the
direction she is paving is of her own making.
Empowered by her choices, she came upon the
embankment- where her jaguar helped her climb
out of the water.

They found a cave- she entered because she
finally felt brave.

The Gladiator and The Lion Man

When she stepped into the cave, was she really
that brave?
Before she could think it through the interior
rearranged.
She found herself placed back in time or was it
really in her mind?
In the center of the room stood a towering statue
of a man who waged a crusade to conquer it all.
She panicked in disbelief, pivoting to each side
enclosed in marble slabs with books that covered
the walls.
That is when she heard her Spirit say, "Do not
panic. There is something to live for. Let us not
get lost in this."
And there he was- wrapped in lion's skin held by
a medallion, fashioned from gold with the
emblem of the beast, hanging around his chest.
She felt it in her soul as he stepped closer- it was
clear that her heart was shifting.
The Lion Man's gaze lit a fire within.
He forged wars for beauty but did not want to
recognize her divinity.
It is not that he lacked love for her- it is that he
did not know how to show her.
He built his love with unstable peace.

He doubted her brilliance and his worthiness in
it.
And with every empty word a fighter started to
brew.
The inferior flame grew from within.
Her burning down the potential of what he could
have been.
So she set a blaze to everything that made him
stand tall in his chest.
Every treasure burnt to ashes.
They knew they would not last.
They fell into defeat.
The gladiator's energy was depleted.
She stayed on the ground where she looked
around and there was no sign of him.
She noted the golden weight was in her hand.
She held the lion's head to palm and found an
engraving:
"May God Devour My Enemies."
Her jaguar approached her while she was in
tears- laying on her back.
She absorbed the scars he inflicted.
The marble walls stayed finding themselves in
near pitch black with a few bricks empty from it,
allowing the moon to shine in.
She closed her eyes and thanked her Spirit. Her
Spirit gave her healing strength that the Lion
Man will never know.
She fell asleep letting go of the gold medallion.

The Moon Goddess

Staring at the constellation filled sky daily.
Found herself in the balance of divine
femininity.
Always finding her strength in vulnerability.
A listening goddess that anchors her in the
craters' protection.
The peace that shines down on her, she
surrenders.
Sanctuary and balance from the moon's light.
Moments of sadness substituted for gladness, the
reckless storm meeting a calm wind, and never
abandoned.
A warmth from a goddess blesses her
brokenness and heals her with presence.

The Lost City

The Lost Girl dreamt of where all the lost souls
go to run.
A city luring with beauty- crystals and pearls
embedded into all the walls.
The moment she recognized where she was, she
began to feel her demons approach- so she ran.
How quickly she felt the city pulled her into the
suffocating sand.
What a reminder of what it means to be human.
Are we all bound to a patriarch?
Overwhelmed by the feeling of recognizing her
father left her for this place.
She felt her soul trying to breathe-
Stating, "I am equipped with all that I need."
Her anxiety overwhelming, she ran to the holy
ground where her footing would be solid.
Her spirit told her it was time to leave this place.
But she wished she could just see his face.
Spirit reminded her:
"Have faith that his absence benefited you.
He did all he could even if it wasn't enough.
He trusted you would never be without.
Remember you are the sun.
He encouraged you to see the call to me.

You shine brighter than his darkness, so he
leaves you to be.
Forgive him for me."
So the Sun Girl accepted her gift.
Forgiving the fact that he let his world crumble
at his feet.
Her nightmare came to an end accepting she
could not save him.
The jewel encrusted walls let a few more bricks
fall.
Her eyes opened to the pain of a dream catcher
seared into her skin.
Still stuck inside the cave holding onto her brave
jaguar.

The Death

She thought as she petted his fur, "how much
more of this can I take?"
So she breathed to escape once more.
This time it was an open door.
Too afraid to move forward.

She stated:
"Oh God, how could you be?
You put the pain of a soul in me.
And I stand at a threshold and I do not know
what you expect of me!
Do I step into the depth of knowledge?
The ego is calling me.
It wants and it wants and I do not know what I
can give that will make me want to live.
Immediate gratification has been my suffocation.
I have laid in a bed of disparity.
Please come to me.
I am tired of this anxiety.
I do not know a dream from reality.
I want to move forward in your direction.
But how do I trust your protection?
You let me walk amongst the dead.
How could you think I would have more left?

And now you ask me to walk once more to your
door.
It is tiring, wanting your dream.
You want the woman I am capable of being.
So help me fuel my passion because I am done
screaming.
Be beside me, so I may lay my head low.
So just let me fall, I will just leave this crystal.
I'm tired of being in this catalyst.
I know I am magic, just give me a chance.
I'm all of me- even in my beliefs that you made
it all to communicate with me.
I promise to drop things for your divine
protection but it may take me sometime to learn
certain lessons.
Know when I step it is not my intent to fall or is
that a lie, so I do not even have to try?
Just be my guardian for all that I am, even in my
choices guide me to listen and move in your
permission.
Why are you asking me to be brave?
To walk amongst a grave again- to speak your
word and be true to my Spirit.
Why do you ask for me to chase my dreams?
If this is what you want, then stand beside me.
Let me take it all in.
I'll be your discipline.
Stop putting me in the upper room.

So that I may move once more to be guided by
you.
Stand beside me, as I untangle my discord of
what I'm trying to do.
I will let go of my past if that is what it takes.
I'll shine like the sun like you've created me to
be.
I understand there is maná but that is just the
landscape.
What I'm capable of being.
Everytime I am in the sky.
It is for us to embrace.
I am asking for your grace."

So she felt herself make a move toward the door.
A heart's valve opened once more.

Spirit

Spirit says:

Have a conversation with God daily.
Have love for yourself.
The meaning of life is God, family, and the joy
in your being when you surrender to the
moment.
Enjoy the present.
Do not fear.
Pursue your wildest dreams.
Dance with me daily.
Write to me and laugh.
Believe in yourself.
Have confidence in your being.
Hold honesty first.
Help others.
Give up time for payment of kind.
Build your body.
Question your feelings.
Listen to me often.
Understand you are not every thought.
Hold up your unconditional love.
Let that sink in.
Do not forget to move swiftly to let your peace
in.

Walls

Boundaries-
She is willing to compromise in safety, in trust,
and in patience.
Find romance within her life.
Learning her worth and beauty.
Her soul will be sound.
Patient in peace.
Her love has value.
She will never forget her soul's name.
Stepping into intuition faster.
She will remember to be mindful of her
reflection in a relationship.
Push for her growth will bring her solutions to
things she has felt were problematic.
Peace and gratitude is what she finds hope in
daily.
Nothing else is needed because spirit saved her.

Rose Garden

She stepped into the rose garden.
It has a whimsical enchantment.
The ground at her feet, she begins to heal.
The sweet scent of agape is here.
To be in a sanctuary with the blessing of a rose.
The sweet little rose is a reminder of what is
entrusted in her- the gift of hearing flowers.
Profound finite enjoyment.
What grows from the ground can be the friend
she needs in solitude.
With flowers there's nothing to prove.
All the more reason to understand that it just
takes time to bloom.
In the enchanted garden, a single white butterfly
flew by- she began to follow its soar.

The Butterfly Girl

The girl was given wingsbecause she trusted
God.
She surrendered her being to follow His literal
word for word meaning.
The living word she breathes in.
The Lost Girl knew she was so confused with
why she felt like the butterfly girl had something
different with the creator.
How she flew amongst life trusting God would
save her.
Within His being He would carry her just so she
knew there was meaning.
Finding time to put in with the divine is found in
many places but the Butterfly Girl knew what
the Lost Girl liked to stay in.
Accept a love without any condition that's a
bond that outweighs anything new.
The Sun Girl continued to walk remembering
she was no longer lost.

.

The Wings

With each placement of her sole a searing pain
grew in the blades of her back.
With the cold winds came the pain.
Her trying to remember what had happened to
be so directed.
She let an image of beautiful feathering wings
cascaded down her back come to mind.
But the recollection did not last for too long.

Confirmation

She has this vision while she follows the beat in her rhythm.
Of the Butterfly Girl standing across from her without any wings in the cold of the ocean.
Guardians standing on each side of them preparing them to be still in their being. The Sun beamed at the Butterfly.
Their gaze into each other's eyes locked in.
Surrendering to the tide was about to begin.
Silent goodbyes felt between two girls that knew God wanted something different for them.
They stared with fierce love until their bodies were tipped back.
Washing all away.
Waves swaying them to take a breath.
Stuck in the deepest love.
Anointed.

The Earth and the Dragon

The Sun Girl walked along the shore of the
planet.
Trying to find how to befriend it.
As she continued to walk there was a Dragon.
She thought it was there to defend her being.
But in her recognition, her instinct enlisted her
to find the tree that would bring her peace.
The dragon she could tell was different because
he flooded the land with watery emotions.
And everyone that stood on it was left
speechless .
Trust in her being- she set forth to find how she
could help Mother Earth continue to live within
God's protection.
She felt the Dragon's waters could be confused
as a curse.
His emotions are there to just point out what
hurts.
He too loves Mother Earth.

Native Love

She came across another creative- he was a
native.
He felt safe so she proceeded; naked in fragility.
He tried to teach her how to stand tall.
He exhausted her with the reminders of her fall.
And he left her with dismantled thoughts.
Recognizing he could have her just in the splits
of her disconnects.
He would state, "It is okay to just be living."
That is how he loves-
He reminded her of peace until she felt his
unwillingness to trade.
A familiarity she knew all too well.
So she said, "goodbye" to the native's tongue to
be built in her own love.

Ministry

Not every step is made while being brave.
Some moves are made with false intentions.
The dust in her mind has officially settled.
She was finding some sense of worth.
She started to recognize the reality of every
single sign that was created for another lover.
Every emotional tactic to get what was wanted
from a twining situation.
And it crumbled in her hands.
Never again wanting to be this way-
A hurtful lover lurks within a soul creating
emotional manipulation.
She realized that there is so much growth to be
had from the experience of knowing false hope
is not enough.
She can't hold on to a lover's presence in her life
if it isn't providing healthy dynamics on how to
love properly.
The lover always wants the upper hand.
It will always put lust first at the expense of her
growth.
She will let her idea of love be an ideal.
She just wants love of self and to forgive this
moment especially because it grew her to
examine her being.

So she prayed and walked upon the earth where
she found an abandoned church.
What a familiarity- another threshold she had
come up on.
As soon as she walked through the falling doors,
wings grew from her back and cascaded to the
floor.
This place was not even a dream.
She knew she had been here before.
A memory.
She walked up to the altar that stood in front of a
ledge to the ocean.

And that is when she saw the imprint on time.
Where the Butterfly Girl and the Native Love
ripped the Sun Girl's wings off.
They said it was done out of love.
She saw herself cry out in defeat.
An affair she felt did not make her divinity that
weak.
The two she thought she knew pulled her to the
ledge and pushed her off.
In shock- she held her jaguar in disbelief.
She thought:
"Was this what happened to me?

I lost sight of my creativity.
I stepped against another being without
recognizing my reptilian lover inside."

She had experienced enough of her past.
She came to this door to find a tree that holds
wisdom for her to ask.

The Forgiving Tree

She walked through the garden of the hallowed
ground until she found a tree standing tall and
proud.
She sat up against it laying her legs in front of
her.
The jaguar tired of the journey laid upon her like
a pillow.
She did her best to stay still.
Another place she felt like she could take rest
after finding out her discord stemmed in not
trusting God's plan.
So she slept.
Trying to accept forgiveness.

The Elephant Chief

She woke to a flame approaching her in the
chaos of night.
She stared at another being walking closer.
This one was much older.
Wise enough to create a fire in front of her to
provide warmth.
He silently waited for her to ask her first
question.
She asked at the tree of knowledge all night.
Her chief tattooed an elephant at the side of her
foot so that he walked any which way she
moved.
Before he left, he spoke, "you did not ask the
biggest one of them all."
She stayed quiet only for a moment, "Do you
think God still loves me in my missteps?"

He held her close and simply stated,
"Do not let your soul become this jaded.
Our tribe needs you to grow beyond acceptance
of what others may think.
God is not a native or a butterfly.
He created us to see the value of our being, so
that we may create to.

Do not allow yourself to forget your gift of
empathy.
That is why you have come across so many
trails.
Having unconditional love for self is hard to
progress toward even in the missteps.
God does not make or believe you to be any less
than the Sun who loves to shine on anyone in the
middle of the day.
Do not forget the lineage you came from.
There is no need to defeat something that does
not make you weak.
Stand tall in your steps.
Not all moments define you.
Let your conversation with Him be the one that
guides you.
My sweet girl, are you not tired of being lost?
Forgive it all so that way you start brand new.
Do you not know I only want absolute love for
you?"

He kissed her goodbye.
She hugged him a bit tighter, grateful for his
presence.
The elephant chief reminded her of the ability to
let go of the definitions of her being that do not
serve her.
She fell asleep at the tree once more.

Forever

There is no such thing as forever.
It does not happen in this lifetime.
So when the jaguar and the Sun Girl finally
stepped away from the tree, they stepped with a
resilient pace.
She knew forgiveness happened through her
core.
Her heart grew bigger once more.
She understood with each experience there was
more to explore.
So her and the jaguar stood at the ledge
forgiving the Lost Girl for following her heart.
It was what produced a new start.